The Leader's

Small Handbook of Wisdom Anecdotes

The Leader's Small Handbook of Wisdom Anecdotes

Nuggets That Can Help You Navigate Some of Life's Greatest Challenges

Jocelyn R. Howard

The Citadel of Perpetual Learning
Warren, Michigan

The Leaders Small Handbook of Wisdom Anecdotes
© 2024 Jocelyn R. Howard.

All rights reserved. No part of this publication may be reproduced, distributed, or transmitted in any form or by any means, including photocopying, recording, or other electronic or mechanical methods, without the prior written permission of the publisher, except in the case of brief quotations embodied in critical reviews and certain other noncommercial uses permitted by copyright law. Published in the United States by The Citadel of Perpetual Learning.

Paperback: 979-8-218-48812-3

10 9 8 7 6 5 4 3 2 1
1st Edition, October 2024

Printed in the United States of America

TABLE OF CONTENTS

Foreword vii

Introduction ix

What Day Is It? 1

Who's Counting Anyway? 3

Please Stop Talking 5

Recklessness 9

Speak What You See 13

I Am Listening 17

Who Are You Talking To? 21

Lights, Camera, Action 25

What Is Old Is New 29

I Am Sorry Your Honor 33

I Can't See That Far 37

Why Did You Do That? 41

Work Is Hard 47

Who Said That? 51

The Wrong Gear 55

Pay Attention..59

I Am Not a Party of One...61

What a Joy To Be Loved..65

Can I Help You?..69

Who's Afraid of the Big Bad Wolf?...............................73

Did I Hear You Correctly?...79

Just Stop It...83

Do You Have A Band-aid?...87

What Time Are You Getting Up?..................................91

I Am Going Where You're Going..................................95

I Want to Be Where You Are....................................... 101

Wisdom Quotes.. 105

FOREWORD

The Leader's Small Handbook of Wisdom Anecdotes

As a pastor of a thriving ministry, I met Jocelyn Howard in church several years ago and immediately found that she was a person who loved helping people. I found out later that she was an educator and loved traveling, so I asked her to be on the executive board of our church. I soon realized that she had a calling on her life much larger than just our church, but to touch many more lives outside the church, so I asked her to be the church's community relations director to our city. Since then, she has brought together many city officials, leaders, and students to do many wonderful city events to unite and serve the community. She also was chairperson of the planning commission for our city.

Jocelyn Howard has helped many people, including myself, to understand the importance of living together in a community where everyone matters regardless of their economic status, race, gender, religion, or political affiliation. The short accounts she tells of her personal life are filled with wisdom that will bless any reader whether you're a leader or not. You don't have to start at the beginning of this handbook, you can open this book at any point on any page and find inspiration, and instructions for everyday living.

She is certainly qualified not only academically, but her experience in life with real people, young and old; people of diverse backgrounds and cultures in real situations allows her to articulate with clarity and humor the wisdom she's gained.

She shares her insights with personal testimonies, missteps, and lyrics of songs that will warm your heart and inspire you.

To get deeper into the insights of wisdom through living life with your eyes wide open, I suggest you begin reading this handbook right away.

Bishop Adolphus L. Cast
Founder and Pastor Emeritus,
LAM Christian Church

INTRODUCTION

The year 2020 was like no other year in my lifetime. However, I would be foolish to think that I am the only person, or this is the only time that there has been a crisis. Once COVID-19 hit the shores of the United States, I instinctively looked for someone who may have lived during the last pandemic. I wanted to know how they handled a crisis, and what things I should be looking out for. During my search, I realized that all of my resources had passed away. My grandmother, Maggie Moore, had died six years previously at the ripe old age of 103; and my great aunt Zenolia Butler had died three years previously at the age of 106. These resources would have been a guiding light for me and many others on how to navigate this crisis. However, no one in my immediate circle was able to shed light on how to live through a crisis of biblical proportions. Instead, there were so many voices, so many opinions, so much information, and misinformation. There was so much information that any rational person would be nauseous about information overload. Because information without proper interpretation is deadly. My pastor, Bishop Adolphus Cast is often quoted as saying, "Information without application leads to frustration."

I have always been one who seeks counsel from those who are older, and I earnestly believe that the answers that we so desperately seek are found primarily in a person not necessarily in research. Because wisdom is to be lived, not so much read. The wisdom that is applied and practiced in our daily lives will lead to practical experience. My thoughts can never be the loudest in my head, rather these should be thoughts that are buffered through the annals of time and secured by their longevity. I earnestly believe that some of the missteps in life have occurred because we have tried to recreate what has already been proven. The propensity of a generation has been not to seek understanding, but to try to recreate, reinvent, and dismiss. In doing so, we have built systems on errors, unproven hypotheses, and emotional tantrums. But I would rather believe that applying proven systems and patience of wisdom which will create a healing salve, will cement solutions that are applicable for generations to come.

So hence began my journey. With the nudging of a good friend, Janet Platt, she convinced me to keep a journal by my bed and to write passages and thoughts that guided me through one of the darkest seasons of a century. The quotes that I'm going to provide to you are not thoughts of by me. Rather, it's me stilling myself long enough to hear a still small voice of God in a season with so much chatter. These guiding thoughts comforted me in a very dark season; yet brought hope, peace, joy, awareness, and expectation. I don't purport to be a writer at this moment; what I am is just a scribe. I am merely sharing with you thoughts that God has given me, and I hope they will be a blessing to you. The thoughts are in no particular order or theme, they are merely God's thoughts crafted through the annals of time to a mere mortal who listened to what He was saying.

WHAT DAY IS IT?

July 29, 2020 entry:"It is an amazing power to open up one day and close another."

The home delivery and Amazon age have become part of our everyday existence. The number of corrugated boxes that are in our daily existence is breathtaking. If you drive down any neighborhood now you see a sight that was once relegated to just special deliveries in years past; instead, you see porches full of boxes. Uniquely, there can be multiple deliveries per day from varying vendors carrying items from food to footwear.

Yet, it is more amazing that there are 365 days in a calendar year. However, each day has tremendous significance, in that it holds so much power, sadness, joy, commitment, and potential. Yet all of that is packaged in one 24-hour day. There is so much that can be done in a day, yet when the day is over it is done. But who is responsible for closing out the day at 11:59 p.m., and opening a new day at midnight?

Please notice that it is not a "re-opening" but a new opening. That old day must be packaged up, tucked in, shelved, and packed in the box of history. The new day must be opened and delivered with care to all the citizens of the world. What was in yesterday and what is in today must be seamlessly done at the same time! Closing and opening must be done simultaneously, and only God can handle such a delicate and powerful task.

Our life is in His hands, and He alone knows our days, i.e., our beginning and end, and the days in between. Yet, His amazing balance between yesterday and today is done in a second! It begins and ends. But He is there continuously, daily, weekly, monthly, annually, throughout ages without a single interruption in the plan. The sheer power to do both at the same time is unimaginable without comparison. Yet He does it without assistance from anyone. There is never an issue or a supply chain shortage. Rather, this process is so immaculate in its precision that we can overlook its power of it.

God knows that whatever is going to be accomplished or not accomplished He has given us 24 hours by which to do it, and He tucks it away in history. Yet, He also provides all that we need to carry over into a new day. He is so ever mindful of us as we trust Him for our daily bread.

"Blessed be the Lord who daily loadeth us with benefits."
(Psalms 68:19)

WHO'S COUNTING ANYWAY?

July 8, 2020 entry:"God can do in a day what would take us years"

I can clearly remember my high school days in Detroit. I can remember the grand hallways, the elevators, the green and white school colors, and our athletic teams. I remember riding public transportation going back and forth to school, and I remember clearly my graduation day. Our K-12 education is somewhat of an incubator for young people. You can go to school and your first memory is taking a nap in kindergarten and before you know it, you're walking across the stage with tassels, a cap, and a gown. In my mind, it seems like everything after that is a sprint to the finish line. For whatever reason days fold into weeks, months into years, and the ability to chart your progress can seem like a moving target. Growing up I had a favorite soap opera, which was, The Days of Our Lives; and the theme was: 'Like sand in an hourglass so are the days of our lives."

However, there is nothing like the presence of God where there is neither time nor space. He has a unique ability to transport us in His presence where the outer world doesn't seem to matter as much. There are no deadlines, meetings, emails, or pressing agendas. Where He is there is joy, peace, comfort, tranquility, agelessness, and anti-time or timelessness. You see time was marked and created for man to identify days and years. But with God, He can just do one thing, and immediately it has an eternal effect. Not only does what He says affect our current state, but it travels to accomplish both past and future implications. Without opposition, everything must fall in place to His desire. His Word stretches across the Milky Way of decisions and past mistakes. And He can do this in an instant…and it is permanent. We toil for years with charts, graphs, metrics, and algorithms and sometimes with only measured success. But with God, He can change an entire trajectory of your life in just a simple encounter in one day.

Who's counting anyway…

PLEASE STOP TALKING

November 17, 2020 entry: "We can only speak so many words because our intelligence quotient is only so much. But if they are anointed words they can break through any situation."

I am a lover of words! But more importantly, I like words from a different time or a different culture. I like words in different languages, and I like discovering ancient meanings of words. I just like words! However, the overuse of words is quite annoying to me. And I dislike it when a certain phrase or word is given a brand-new meaning just for a cultural whim.

I remember some years ago I was traveling as a road manager with a gospel artist, and I had the wonderful privilege of going to Birmingham, England. Now Birmingham is a working man's town, where all the city workers lived and then commuted into London, England. We traveled in December, and it was cold and blustery and full of rain and cloudy skies. Yet the town was full of old-world charm, character, etiquette, and refined decorum. It was well understood that there was to be no waste, nor overstepping your station in the community.

Every worker was very much aware of their prescribed occupation, and they performed their duties with class and distinction.

As we were out in the town one day, I made the awful mistake of bringing a hot cross bun into a coffee shop to get some hot chocolate. The proprietor was up in arms and yelling and screaming at me about my lack of tact in bringing another merchant's goods into his store. He was causing such a scene that I was extremely embarrassed and was about to walk out of the store. The gospel artist that I was with walked up to him and said this simple phrase. I thought she was going to tell him we were tourists, and he wasn't behaving in a friendly manner. However, she simply said, "shhhhhh you're talking too loud!" For whatever reason that simple phrase caused him to calm down, apologize, and invite us to sit down to have something warm to drink in his establishment with my hot crossed bun still in tow.

We are living in a world that is full of words but not full of anointed words. Because it doesn't matter how many words you speak if they don't have the power and conviction to change a situation. Words for word's sake is mere babble, it's baby talk with no cohesiveness or authority. But a word fitly spoken is like apples of gold on platters of silver; it's descriptive and thought-provoking. It's alive and is a transporter. It demands a confrontation of the status quo! It provides the stimulus for change, a call to action with a targeted goal in mind. Our intellect doesn't produce change, anointing does. Can someone tell them to stop talking?

Leader's Self-Reflection

Identifying Your Current Mindset: Having the Last Word

Reflection is the first step in understanding where you currently stand. Here are a series of questions aimed at helping you identify your mindset:

1. Are you a person who shares conversation time or do you consume most of the conversation?

2. In an honest assessment, why do you feel the need to be right in a situation?

3. Based on the last entry, find 3 ways that you can alter your posture in a conversation to allow for more listening than responding.

RECKLESSNESS

July 6, 2020 entry: "recklessness is doing whatever I want to do"

I have never considered myself to be artistic. I am hard-pressed to draw a proficient stick man. My drawing and art capacity has always been limited, and quite frankly not very impressive. Some years ago, a friend of mine introduced me to an art studio called Creative Arts. This art studio allowed us to paint pottery, work with mosaics, and paint on canvases. This exercise in artistic expression was very challenging for me because I had never mastered Art. But I discovered that being in that studio was very relaxing, and engaging, and allowed me to explore a side of me that was dormant. I discovered that Art has its own set of rules, though it may seem very freestyle and random. It seems uninhibited, but this is far from the truth; every artist still works within the borders of what is acceptable. Certain paints are not conducive for certain mediums, and some instruments can only be used on particular exteriors. Triangles, circles, hexagons, trapezoids, and cubes only intermingle with correct precision. I was beginning to like this art thing!

See, I believe the real reason I didn't like art was that it felt very reckless, and without order. Part of my personality is structure. Now, I'm not a stuffed shirt, but I like things to make sense. If it's too imaginative it can be a bit creepy to me. However, what I noticed was there was order and precision to the process, even if it was messy.

I believe my apprehension of art was the messiness. Yet the messiness is not recklessness. Recklessness operates with no intended goal in mind besides chaos. It is the notion that I can do whatever I want whenever I want to without regard for intended or certain harm. There will not be a concern for the harm to the person or others impacted by your decision. Recklessness never colors within the lines, neither does it follow the connect the dots to create an image on a canvas. It has no regard for the color palette or the mixing of water-based versus oil-based paint. Instead, recklessness takes all the paint, mosaics, pottery wheels, and ceramics and puts them in a blender, and tells us to like them. Recklessness dares the onlooker to critique their work; is hostile to correction; has no regard for the medium that they are trampling upon; and doesn't own the results of their work.

The earth is full of art from the mountains to the valleys, from the oceans to the islands that set up on them. Yet they operate with cohesiveness because they respect their individual boundaries. Our lives must be chartered outside of the realm of recklessness. We cannot do whatever we want to do whenever we want to do it without certain calamity. I discovered that art allowed me to be creative without being destructive. Let's live our life accordingly.

SPEAK WHAT YOU SEE

January 1, 2021 entry: "A vision is not a vision unless you can articulate it, otherwise it's a scheme (private) only for a few and you."

For over 20 years I have been a corporate trainer in varying industries; from education to automotive, and from health care to social services and there is one question that is paramount in any industry. What is your vision? As a service provider, I am tasked with helping companies achieve or motivate them to push toward their goal. The assignment of helping is never the problem. The team that I work with is extremely gifted and full of great and innovative ideas. Once we are contracted to do work, we put boots on the ground ready to accomplish the project assigned to us. Every assignment given to us is solely a challenge for us to become more creative; by discovering methods that have not been employed before, thus solving problems.

The truth of the matter is that I love what I do! I love helping people achieve their goals. The caveat to my work is trying to get industry leaders to tell me what their vision is. I am not suggesting that they are not good leaders.

But straightforwardly, if there is any question that seems to befuddle industry leaders it is, "what is your vision?" I find this extremely disturbing because the industries that seem to have the greatest difficulty answering this question are companies that deal with people. Industries that are manufacturing a product will quickly share with me some keen targets: get to market faster, eliminate waste, produce a friendly work environment, etc. However, organizations that deal with people—the most precious commodity have the most difficult time telling me what their vision is. They talk about outcomes that have nothing to do with people. They talk about systems that don't produce outcomes that will benefit the people they are serving. The most heartbreaking aspect is that they are not aware that the work that they are doing is not attached to the people that they are serving. This begs the question: is it a vision or a scheme?

Jack Welch the former CEO of General Electric and master business leader once said: "Good business leaders create a vision, articulate the vision, passionately own the vision, and relentlessly drive it to completion." An organization and its employees need to know where they are going and collectively measure if targets are met. Otherwise, the planning is simply a ruse, a scheme to be changed at any moment to the unexpecting eye. This isn't complex. How many people book a flight, and the expectation (vision) is that they will arrive in Los Angeles; yet you arrive in Topeka, Kansas without notification of the change, or provision to get to your original destination? If this occurs, then it was a scheme all along without consideration of others involved. It's selfish and without pure motivation, with a lack of regard for the people impacted. See, the essence of a vision is the ability to articulate it, express it, massage it, and cause others to imagine it. Without expression, weaving of details, and fluid communication to all, a scheme can disguise itself as a vision.

Leadership requires openness, transparency, and boldness to carve out a green pasture for the people that are being led. This is without compromise. In a society that has an abundance of words and access to so much information, it is baffling that a vision would be hard to articulate. But a vision is not mere words; it's a commitment to people. It's putting all your skin in the game for all to see and measure. It requires a person, institution, or agency to be brutally candid about their commitment to change and improvement. A vision is speaking of what you see, and without sight, there is no vision.

Leader's Self-Reflection

Identifying Your Current Mindset: Vision Casting

Reflection is the first step in understanding where you currently stand. Here are a series of questions aimed at helping you identify your mindset:

1. Write concisely what your vision is for your business, non-profit, ministry, or organization.

2. What do you want your organization to be known for 30 years from now?

3. How do you plan to ensure the institutional integrity of the organization after you leave? In other words, what are you doing to ensure that certain principals remain in tact?

I AM LISTENING

June 26, 2020 entry: "God articulates Himself in nature-do your work to let people know that you are God."

I've never considered myself an outdoorsy person, yet I love being in nature. I love the rolling hills of Jackson Hole, Wyoming, and the swift breeze off Lake Jefferson in Washington, or the azure color of the eastern Mediterranean ocean, or the sunrise in Maui. All these locations are breathtaking, producing a great sense of awe, and causing me to try to capture these moments eternally in my memory. Each location has its distinctive characteristic, without impeding or competing with the other locations. The range of colors, valleys, mountains, rivers, and wildlife all write their scripts in the book of nature. It is breathtaking to absorb it and to know that you have no control over its origin or end.

I clearly remember March 13, 2020; it's when Governor Whitmer of Michigan and so many other governors shut their states down due to COVID-19. We were all sheltered in place in our homes unless we were given special documentation that we were essential workers. I remember the eerie quietness that surrounded my subdivision and local streets. I remember that there were possibly only 3-4 cars on the road every 15-20 minutes, versus 50-100 cars every minute. It was a chilling reality that millions upon millions of people were shut in their homes. I also recall how the days were so long, with no superfluous activities to fill our day. On the other hand, I did notice an activity that had purpose and continuity.

As I looked out my kitchen window every day around 3:17 pm, I would see a cardinal sitting on the maple tree chirping away. Before I could look away, I would see their playful behavior with a set of robins. To my amazement, this happened every day at 3:17! I then said to myself, "is this what is going on around here while I am at work? This playfulness in my backyard is delightful!" I began to watch their banter every day, but also their work because they were building a nest to prepare for the new babies that would be arriving. Then, I noticed the buds on the trees, the blades of grass springing forth, rabbits hopping, and flowers pushing through the soil, and the pandemic could not prevent the awesome articulation of God. God was speaking, and His words were decorated in beauty and majesty. The sky radiated color, and every rainfall reminded me that there were more raindrops than anyone could ever capture in a bucket.

The time that produced so much grief was also a time when we had the opportunity to see God's amazing voice. His expressiveness in nature demands our attention in that

He weaves a collection of blues and greens, then He adds a whisk of white and purple. It's so robust that we can only capture sections in our brain at a time because we cannot consume all the kaleidoscopes of colors.

God cannot deny the fact that He exists, and His creation explodes and screams for us to pay attention to see how articulate He is.

WHO ARE YOU TALKING TO?

August 9, 2020 entry: "There is a difference between counsel and wise (seasoned) counsel. Some counsel you can't take because it isn't aged."

Is it me or are there a lot of personal injury attorneys with television commercials these days? During this season, it leaves me to inquire if there are scores of people getting injured, or are we more prone to litigate everything? It seems that every commercial is about a personal injury attorney but very few commercials are for plumbers or mechanics. Wouldn't it be reasonable to assume that you would need a plumber or mechanic at least twice per year? Yet, seventy percent of the aired commercials that I have seen have been for litigation. Then I began to wonder how a person would decide whom to choose if they had to litigate: the one who had the best jingle; the most attractive; the trendiest office space; those who had the largest settlements; or the one who has been around the longest.

Counsel can be a tricky subject because counsel is often based on the temperament of the one seeking it. Seemingly, everyone is a street attorney, with just a little bit of experience with the legal system. But that isn't counsel. The antiquity of the profession of counselor is related to the ability to steer or guide, or the management of the ropes. This means that in a difficult, troubled, uncertain, or perplexing time, the engagement of counsel or a counselor can help guide, steer, or take the ropes to produce a settled or calmer outcome. Their profession is to give advice. They have studied, evaluated causes, and tested their validity; and thus devoted their life to the nobility of giving sound advice.

Yet, there is another aspect to counsel, and that is how often it has been used for the desired outcome. Some have become so proficient at their craft that they specialize in the hard cases. Meaning that there are people who have managed crises so often that there are very few predicaments that they are not familiar with. These individuals are seasoned, aged, and full of wisdom that they are like fresh bouquets of flowers. From their lips are drops of understanding that make the most complex cases seem like nursery rhymes. Every word is filled with comfort, peace, direction, and sound advice. This is aged counsel; because whatever the case, the accuracy of its application will yield a positive result. To them they never expend time on the problem, they have learned to foster energy on solutions. Problems are made to be solved, and they are master problem solvers. Their errors have better results than an unwise person's best decision.

Real counselors are not found in TV ads, but they are to be sought out with diligence because they live in antiquity. They live in a space where regardless of if it's 50 years in the past, or 50 years in the future, the advice that they give will produce the desired result. This is because pure seasoned counsel is ageless. In a crisis, seasoned counsel produces comfort like a warm blanket on a cold day. Beware when advice can be purchased versus being sought.

Leader's Self-Reflection
Identifying Your Current Mindset:

Reflection is the first step in understanding where you currently stand. Here are a series of questions aimed at helping you identify your mindset:

1 How do I react when I face a challenge in my personal or professional life? Do I tackle it head-on or shy away? How do I communicate these changes?

2 Do I appreciate feedback and criticism, viewing them as chances to improve? Or do I become defensive and disheartened? Who can I trust to give me honest feedback and criticism?

3 What are my beliefs about my abilities? Do I believe I can grow and change, or am I stuck with what I have? Do I communicate growth strategies to those around me and who I influence?

LIGHTS, CAMERA, ACTION

May 31, 2021 entry: "We talk about a God of order, maybe it's not in the way we think."

I attended a college prep high school growing up, and I must say that my hardest subject in high school was geometry. Geometry always stumped me because unlike other people I do not necessarily see things in three dimensions, I'm somewhat of a flat-image person. As I have shared earlier, even my stick man drawings lack character and shape. Geometry was the only class I failed in high school, and I had to repeat it during summer school. There was something about solving theorems and formulas in geometry. Here is the reason behind my struggle in geometry; I was trying to solve it like an algebraic equation. I wanted to use polynomials and quadratic equations in solving a geometric problem. Well, this approach never worked, and I always ended up failing the assignments. I was frustrated from top to bottom because I could not wrap my head around how to solve the problem.

What ended up happening is in my summer school class I had the most brilliant teacher that unlocked the door to my understanding of geometry. It was like cold water rushing over me on a hot summer day when he unlocked the problem of my understanding. My instructor gave me these simple instructions: "Jocelyn you are trying to solve the equation when you merely have to understand the theorem that associates with the problem." We don't want you to solve it like an algebraic question, we want you to understand what's before you.

Many of us walk through life thinking that God has a specific order by which He does things. Or we feel we feel if we do X Y&Z in a particular order God will be on the very end of that equation. I would like to inject a thought for our consideration: God knows the end from the beginning. While we are attempting to do things in a specific order to get God's response, God always sees the end and works backward. Let me attempt to be a bit more descriptive; we notice the creation story, and man was created on the 6th day. However, I would propose that God always had man in mind first, and then worked backward. Everything that He put first was not necessarily his first intention, rather he was decorating for his ultimate intention. We have struggled in life trying to line up a prescribed order hoping to get the desired result, versus understanding what the desired result should be and then working backward. Too often we spend more time planning than we do understanding. We spent too much time trying to solve it versus understanding what was before us. What I have noticed is we may attempt to plan items out in an attempt to see God at the end of our efforts. Rather than seeing God first, and then adjusting our efforts.

My 10th-grade geometry class taught me a world lesson, it taught me the skill of observation and waiting. Everything may not need to be solved, sometimes the first order of business is to understand.

Leader's Self-Reflection

Identifying Your Current Mindset: Understanding vs Solving?

Reflection is the first step in understanding where you currently stand. Here are a series of questions aimed at helping you identify your mindset:

1 Identify a problem that you have been facing for some time that you have not been able to solve.

2 In an honest approach to your problem, are you trying to solve it or understand it?

3 Based of the current entry, what are 3 things you may have overlooked before trying to solve the problem?

WHAT IS OLD IS NEW

December 14, 2021 entry: "Be careful not to excavate old things until you have somewhere to place them. They are there for your learning, understanding, for our examples."

I love to travel, and I especially love traveling to exotic or ancient cities. In 2010 I took an Eastern Mediterranean cruise, which was by far one of the best vacations that I had taken. Our group traveled to Nice, Barcelona, Sardina, Monaco, and Rome. These cities are rich in history and our excursions were to some of the ancient landmarks that described the history of the city. As we looked at the dates of the monuments and the history, a few things were glaring at me. One, these cities were over 10 centuries old and had sustained many elements of their identity. Two, their history did not erase the wars and battles, whether in defeat or victory. Lastly, the citizens had the presence of mind to preserve, set apart, honor, revere, and maintain the integrity of its cultural heritage. These cities are so steep in the preservation of their history that about any citizen that we spoke to had great pride in the heritage that they possessed by being a part of that region.

However, there was one distinct feature that separated these cities from American cities, American architecture, and the planning and development process. In these cities, it is illegal to tear a building down! Any construction must be done on top of the original structure, or a great part of the original structure must be present in any new expansion. The structure is inextricably tied to history, and history is tied to the event, and the event is tied to the people. So, the dissolution of any of these items has a direct impact on the future sustainability of the region. The provocative thinking of this region is its wealth is not the currency or the GDP (gross domestic product); its currency is its history. This is their defining character. Whether they were conquered or defeated by their enemy, the ancient ruins lecture the listener and tell the story generation after generation. Uniquely, their premises are working because annually hundreds of thousands of tourist flock to these cities just to observe the ancient remains.

I am concerned and would suggest that we temper our desire to always excavate and restart new unfounded methods in our Christian walk. Too often I see new hypothetical spiritual buildings being erected without being attached to an ancient anointing, foundation, or history, which will have a short period because it is not grounded and will be subject to the same principle that it started with, tearing down the old and starting something new. For some reason, there is a current belief that the old and the young cannot operate in the same space. This is a false narrative. This would only be true if we all were timeless and not subject to age. The truth is that we all are aging, and there are more old things in the world than new things. Once a baby is born, a car is driven off the lot, and a house is built; the clock begins to tick, and the aging process begins. Empirically, it is the old that is supporting the new.

The notion of removing landmarks is a false chronicle and is subject to the whims of the immature. I would rather have the landmarks of the past to instruct, guide, and give me an awareness of the things to come. It is this ancient wisdom that sustains generations, and like a well-rooted tree gives shade on a sunny day. I feel compelled to implore us to put down our shovels which seek to uproot the lessons that make us strong.

I AM SORRY YOUR HONOR

*October 25, 2020 entry: "I am not a rule follower,
I am a rule understander."*

I can truthfully attest that I have a clean driving record, but this was not always the case in my embarrassment. While I was in college, I amassed a slew of parking tickets going back and forth to class, well this behavior lent itself to speeding tickets and driving with a suspended license. Yikes! This behavior caused me to be in court for one of my tickets. Before my case was heard a gentleman was before the judge for driving with defective equipment, namely no turn signals. As he was attempting to defend himself and say that the ticket was unwarranted, the judge asked him a series of questions regarding the sound of his turn signals in his vehicle. The query continues and the judge concludes that the defendant knew he had defective turn signals based on the sound that was in his vehicle. But, to add insult to injury, the judge had pulled the defendant's driving history and disclosed that he had outstanding warrants and a history of driving with defective equipment. The man was hauled off to jail and a large bond was set. Needless to say, I ran promptly to the cashier to pay whatever fine was assessed to me without standing before the judge.

In most cases whenever we stand in court or before a person of authority, rarely are we unaware of the reason that we are there. If we don't understand the gravity of the case, we do understand that there was something that preceded us being there. This awareness is needed to defend or shield oneself against persecution. But a better position is to understand the reason for the rule.

During the height of the pandemic, while so many lives were being lost, and individuals were sick, institutions, businesses, and municipalities began to soften or toughen the guidelines or rules that were normally in place before the pandemic. Banks were closed, creditors disregarded late payments, schools and businesses required masks and social distancing, and sterilization was a must. However, while individuals sheltered at home, they also made up their own set of rules. Their self-governance sometimes had a dire impact on the general population once the rules made for self-governance had infringed on others. Please know that I am not speaking about individual rights, those are sacred and respected. I am speaking about understanding why the rule is in place.

The essence of any rule is the unselfish approach to understanding how it impacts the masses. Usually, a rule is put in place because of the infractions of a few that impact multitudes. Hence some look only not to break the rule rather than understand why. My current attempt is to drill down into finding what is the outcome the rule is trying to produce and to maneuver in a space where those boundaries are not crossed. Thus, becoming a rule understander versus a rule follower. For example, if my understanding is that safe and orderly driving is needed to prevent car crashes, then my responsibility as an understander is to drive in a manner that reduces accidents and fatalities. The rule never enters the equation because I am operating above the rule, by achieving its goal. However, if I can't maintain that level, I am subject to being a rule follower.

As Jesus did, He did not abolish the law, He came to fulfill it. I am striving to understand the essence of the issue before it becomes an offense and then a law. By seeking understanding versus punitive actions, we can become better citizens.

Leader's Self-Reflection

Identifying Your Current Mindset: Leadership Style

Reflection is the first step in understanding where you currently stand. Here are a series of questions aimed at helping you identify your mindset:

❶ As a leader, parent, or team member in your honest assessment, are you more reactive in a crisis or do your assess the situation?

❷ Is your behavior predictable to your organization? If, so, what is this behavior?

❸ Name three people in your organization that your decisions will impact immediately? Based on the prior reading, how do you plan to protect them?

I CAN'T SEE THAT FAR

August 26, 2020 entry: "Be careful that you don't limit your exposure, whereby you only hear/see one version of anything"

My father was a chef in the mess hall in the U.S. Navy, and I promise you he was an awesome cook. When you have cooked for hundreds of people, cooking for a family of 7 is very easy. He could make breakfast, lunch, or dinner amazing; and our holiday meals were extraordinary! My siblings have yet to purely capture Dad's peach cobbler, but they are close. He was a master in the kitchen. During our summer vacations, our parents would take us to restaurants and would force us to choose meal options beyond what we were accustomed to. My parents would give us clear guidelines, no hamburgers or chicken strips; we had to choose something that we hadn't had prior, and we all couldn't order the same thing.

It was interesting because even though my father was a great cook, he still exposed his children to other food sources and styles. He wanted his children to appreciate food and style, not just his cooking. He used his cooking just as a platform to build on. I was talking to a friend of mine, and she told me a funny story about a co-worker. She stated that her co-worker refused to let her children eat at other family members' homes. When asked why she stated, "I don't let them eat out anywhere else, so they won't know how bad of a cook I am!"

Proper exposure is part of growth, maturity, and appreciation, and with guidance, one can explore and develop aspects of life that are not found in a singular space. It's difficult to have a conversation with someone who has only a singular or narrow focus, without exposure. I believe that exposure creates an appreciation for what one person is limited to but can be found in another source. Expose means to introduce a person to a new idea, fact, etc. Essentially, it makes the case that it is not encompassed in one thing. But it also implies that we have limited sight and/or reach. Thus, if you are only stimulated by the same stimuli, you will develop a narrow or stunted growth pattern. This can produce an appreciation for one thing and one thing only. Then your ears and eyes only recognize a singular dull sound; you will miss the beauty of harmony of a symphony. I remember my Uncle Bill made a statement to me about someone who was underdeveloped, and he stated, "little girl looks at that man, he thinks he knows everything and that's all he knows."

John Maxwell, the leadership authority is quoted as saying, "A Chinese proverb states, "Behind an able man there are always other able men." The truth is that teamwork is at the heart of great achievement. The question isn't whether teams have value. The question is whether we acknowledge that fact and become better team players. That's why I assert that one is too small a number to achieve greatness. You cannot do anything of real value alone." Therefore, I contend that when we don't allow ourselves new avenues of information flow, we limit our ability to access greatness. Therefore, the telescope of life that is connected by our social interactions is blurred when we don't allow ourselves to be developed by new ideas and people. I've realized that I can't see that far and need just a little bit of help.

WHY DID YOU DO THAT?

May 21, 2021 entry: "It is a lawless person that cannot abide or live within laws that are made; but continues to change laws to fit their propensities.

One area that most people despise is those who cheat. Somewhere their offense irritates the soul of an individual in a way that produces immediate resentment and the need for instant correction. Nothing is worse than running a relay race and someone jumps off the block before the word "go." Or playing a simple game of spades, and the dealer stacks the cards in their favor. Also consider a student who writes the answers to the test in the palm of their hand or some other undisclosed location, only to score higher than the students who studied. Immediately the person who the wrong is leveraged against wants a swift correction to the alleged charlatan.

It is funny that cheating is an universal action that even a child can identify; from an early age, a child can define when someone has gained an unfair advantage over them. It is strange to them when someone has taken their food, doesn't share, or pushed them unfairly. I can recall when I was younger, and I am sure it still plays out today when someone picks up food for a group in a drive-thru, and, they have more french fries than you do. It is abundantly clear that they ate a portion of your fries and gave you the leftovers, while they continue to enjoy their fries to the full. But without any contrition, they are content to have more without replacing what was eaten. The shift in equality of french fry distribution is solely in the hands and heart of the person picking up the food.

So why is this act of cheating so unnerving? I believe this because the center of cheating is lawlessness. It headquarters itself in deceit by giving the illusion that it operates with even-handedness. Rather, it seeks from the very beginning to scheme. Some may beg to differ and contend that it's seeing and advancing an opportunity; that it is the survival of the fittest and the best man wins. I would counter this statement with the belief that very few people willingly give up their advantage to another without discussion first. Wouldn't it be easier to discuss your actions than deceive them? I would also contend that lawlessness is rooted in the premise of taking someone off guard, upending them while they are not looking, throwing dust in their eyes while they are running, and tripping them when they walk. There is a superficial reasoning of being quicker to the draw; but it's a reshuffling of the deck, changing of the rules, shifting the light, and resetting the goal line without sharing that information with the other party.

Unfortunately, lawlessness is directly opposed to honesty. These two cannot occupy the same space. If you're lawless you're not honest, and if you're honest you're not lawless. Honesty roots itself in consideration and appreciation of others, while lawlessness centers itself on self. Its' fuel is how it benefits self (a few), while constantly re-writing the storyline of many. Honesty and truth appreciate the integrity of the moment and those who are in it. It doesn't seek to rewrite rules when the rules are only in place because honor, truth, and integrity exist.

It has always intrigued me how babies could identify cheating. I believe that they have an expectation that we are supposed to be nice, caring, and fair. So, in the words of a child, "Why did you do that?"

Leader's Self-Reflection
Identifying Your Current Mindset: Consideration

Reflection is the first step in understanding where you currently stand. Here are a series of questions aimed at helping you identify your mindset:

1 As a leader are there unique privileges that are afforded to you? If so, what are they?

2 As a leader how do you celebrate, empower, encourage, and advance others in light of your unique privileges?

3 Identify a person in your organization that you know that you need to empower more. Within 1 week, celebrate them publicly and take them to lunch.

Standing on the Promises

Standing on the promises of Christ my King,
Through eternal ages let His praises ring,
Glory in the highest, I will shout and sing,
Standing on the promises of God.

Refrain:
Standing, standing,
Standing on the promises of God my Savior;
Standing, standing,
I'm standing on the promises of God.

Standing on the promises that cannot fail,
When the howling storms of doubt and fear assail,
By the living Word of God I shall prevail,
Standing on the promises of God.

Standing on the promises I now can see
Perfect, present cleansing in the blood for me;
Standing in the liberty where Christ makes free,
Standing on the promises of God.

Standing on the promises of Christ the Lord,
Bound to Him eternally by love's strong cord,
Overcoming daily with the Spirit's sword,
Standing on the promises of God.

Standing on the promises I cannot fall,
List'ning every moment to the Spirit's call,
Resting in my Savior as my all in all,
Standing on the promises of God.

©1886 Russell K. Carter

WORK IS HARD

February 18, 2021 entry: "We are living in a generation which is not measured by impact through work but by pseudo influence."

As a former trainer in the automotive industry, seeing a car assembled on an assembly line is an amazing sight. From the unpainted steel frame moving to the insertion of doors, hoods, seats, and components, this happens in just a matter of minutes. I stood in amazement knowing that what I saw being assembled would be in someone's driveway in a matter of weeks. The ability to create or construct anything triggers an unmatched euphoria. Because of our God-nature, we are designed to make, build, design, construct, imagine, and produce something in life. This idea of building is instinctive and intrinsic to a child. Early on we can see skills displayed in young children where we label them engineers, cooks, designers, mechanics, teachers, and astronauts. Children will manifest early an outward ability and curiosity that is not taught, it is intuitive, and they just do it. Without a textbook or a course, a child's noticeable gift will be apparent; and with proper guidance, they will be able to fulfill those visible talents.

Over the years we have been taught about great inventors and their discoveries. These inventions have modernized our times in addition to simplifying our lives. In our modernized world, we live with the convenience of electricity, indoor plumbing, transportation, and forced heat. We dare not speak about modern search engines which often reduce the need for libraries or encyclopedias; any question that we have is merely a few clicks away. However, each convenience comes with a price.

I would contend that as each modern convenience assumes a part of our lives, it also diminishes our creativity. It also stifles grit, hard work, and/or thinking and pondering. I will not be the first to say that I believe that we have become lethargic, and any appearance of a struggle is met with a swift decision of, "I quit." Please understand that I greatly appreciate our modern amenities, but not at the risk of my brain cells. I can distinctly remember before my smartphone, easily memorized over 60 telephone numbers, and now I only store a percentage of that. So where is creativity and where is our imagination? When do we play in the sand and make sandcastles? Where are the countless hours spent outside making up games with our friends? They are long gone and replaced with what I call pseudo-influence.

I contend that our overindulgence in amenities and lack of natural curiosity have left us trying to influence people without a product. Gone is the idea of allowing the product to speak of our creativity and ingenuity; rather, let me influence negatively or positively the essence of anything without the hard work of putting my hands to it. I am concerned that the dependence on technology will truncate longevity due to the rapid speed with which we utilize it. It has been said that talk is cheap, and I would contend that in the age of social media talk is cheaper than ever before. Because the attention span of our current age is in minutes not months. We are so easily distracted that we cannot concentrate on any topic for more than a day before another topic is presented to us. So, a person's opinion on anything is fleeting at best, and their influence is now focused on someplace else. However, creativity requires a person's hands to get dirty in the process, and residue is left on the skin and surface. This residue is tangible, and it has a life beyond what we say because it will speak for you. You rarely see a farmer influencing his crop, rather the crop speaks about the farmer, and it will tell the story. Work is hard, but the results are lasting. In our era of simplicity and convenience let's not exchange our God-essence of producing for just talking with little results.

WHO SAID THAT?

February 28, 2020 entry: "People are just reciting information without understanding the information."

"Row, Row, Row Your Boat"

Row, row, row your boat,

Gently down the stream.

Merrily, merrily, merrily, merrily,

Life is but a dream.

Row, Row, Row Your Boat is a staple nursery rhyme that has been around for centuries and millions of children have recited these words. As in most nursery rhymes, there's always an underlying moral to the story. In this instance, the moral is don't give up, keep pushing and keep rowing because it will get better as you go. There were more nursery rhymes than anything else in kindergarten because they were instilling life principles in us at a very early age through a safe method. This is also true of Biblical parables which we were taught that a parable was an earthly story with a heavenly meaning. Throughout our adolescence, it seems that my generation was inundated with these examples of personal growth.

As I have gotten older the lessons are more direct and less lyrical, yet I can tie the life event to a nursery rhyme or an adage. The older people in my life always had an analogy or moral story to direct my decisions and to explain why the events were happening. It was unbelievable how they were able to interpret, direct, unravel, and console you in life's ills, and leave you with nuggets to live by. On countless occasions, I have also found myself repeating those same adages to others because they are transferable! In addition, I am conveying the philosophies also because through the ages they have worked.

Yet, I am observing a section of people who like to recite information without an understanding of the doctrines behind the statements. I can understand why this is a compelling trend. Information and ideologies are valuable to the human experience, people will search high and low for answers or solutions to problems. The holders of this information are always highly esteemed and in demand. So, to repeat information is always alluring, however, information without understanding is just a hollow box. What made ancient wisdom so valuable is the holders of the information knew their way around the circumstances. It is similar to a chef in the kitchen, they understand cooking so all they need are the utensils to create a great meal. The ingredients are secondary to the outcome, it will be good. Whatever ingredients they have will have to yield to the mastery of their skill; they are accustomed to cooking. So, it is with those who have wisdom and understanding, they understand their way around a problem.

Can I tell you how you can identify if a person is just repeating the information or understanding the information? You will know the difference if they can tell you what to do if the first option doesn't work, meaning they can always give you a second option immediately that will work in case the first option doesn't. They have a catalog full of experiences tied to solutions. A clear example is when someone can tell you how to navigate traffic without a GPS, they are so familiar with their city that by memory and familiarity, they can navigate you to your destination. They are not unnerved by the traffic; they have mastered it and know the detours. This is how you can detect someone who is reciting versus someone who knows, they have calmness amid a storm, they know the exit ramp, and how to deliver you safely. Currently, I'm noticing a lot of recitation but not a lot of understanding.

Who's rowing the boat?

THE WRONG GEAR

March 21, 2021 entry: "When you feel a start and stop and no progress in your life it's because we're doing the work, and we are in the way. Move out the way and allow God to move and you'll see progress."

There is nothing like the thrill of driving a manual transmission vehicle. The ability to guide and shift the vehicle and to weave strategically through traffic is exhilarating. My first car was a Toyota Corolla GTS red 2-door coupe, and she was a fireball. It was a delight to traverse the city and highway with ease. It was a fun car. However, anyone who has driven a stick shift can tell you that if you're inexperienced in driving a manual car you can strip the gears.

The lesson that I learned about driving a manual vehicle is that the engine maxes out at a certain speed and the driver has to gear up, or gear down. But if you don't shift and adjust the gear at the same time the car will stall. Often many drivers will take the car back to the first gear to start the process again, and some have said that the 3rd gear is the hardest one to adjust. But all stick shift drivers know if you can get out of 3rd gear that 4th and 5th gears are a breeze.

This is a simple analogy of our lives. God should always be in control of our lives and charting our path. But seemingly as humans, we interject ourselves in God's plan and push the accelerator when He is braking or begin to brake when He is accelerating. In each case, we can cause a stall in the process which can lead to frustration. The worst thing to experience while riding in a car with a manual transmission is perpetual and violent jerking and jolting because the car is in the wrong gear. This lurching is an indicator that the car is not in gear. So, in our spiritual walk, could it be if there is lurching that we are out of step with God? Could our lack of progress, change in mood, cloudy vision, or multiple design changes be a result of us not allowing God to lead?

Each life is designed with ebbs and flows like a sine graph with ups and downs, thus producing a rhythm of our life which over time can produce some level of consistency. Now, this is not an absolute pattern, but for many this is true. But one thing is constant, if God is in our lives, we can see Him at work, He is undeniable and apparent. Conversely, the same is true when He is absent. The absence of God requires way too much human effort which creates man-made results and outcomes. But let me be clear, trouble is not necessarily a gauge that God is not present, because the scripture says that "God is our refuge and strength a very present help in trouble." (Psalms 46:1) However, there is a difference between the absence of God and the presence of man. Because as humans we always mess things up and we create messes. God speaks to messes and designs order and purpose. Yet, when there is more of man than there is of God, we see destruction, confusion, misalignment, and misfiring. We notice stagnant growth and quasi-insight. But notice that even in trouble, a person who is directed by God's plan and timing in confidence will attest that, "God will make a way somehow!" This statement declares that God is leading, and their trust and confidence is in His pacing and desired outcome.

God sets the pace for our lives and our acceleration can be found in our willingness to follow hard after Him and His ways. Let's enjoy the ride and allow Him to lead.

PAY ATTENTION

February 3, 2021 entry: "Pay Attention"

The instructions were very clear. Pay attention. That's all. That's it. Pay Attention.

The rest of this page is left blank intentionally.

I AM NOT A PARTY OF ONE

March 21, 2021 entry: "Watch out for the spirit of secularism versus sanctification. It seeks our will not God's."

Let's begin with a few disclosures. First, I am not an expert on secularism, humanism, agnosticism, pluralism, or liberal philosophies. I am not taking this moment or space to debate the nuance of each or how it has played into society for hundreds of years. Secondly, I won't take this space to dabble in the varying personalities that ascribe to this philosophy. Lastly, this small space is not one of debate of the human mind or propensities. That's not the heart of this small writing.

The heart of this entry is the heart of God and His jealousy for us. I will attempt to describe sanctification versus secularism from a spiritual perspective. Sanctification is merely being set apart for a different and special use. It is difficult to express this in 21st-century thinking because so many rituals and customs have lost their significance. As a kid, I remember the china bureau that held fine china plates and pure silver flatware. We polished the silverware and washed the glasses that were so pristine with either gold or silver rims around the glass lip. We added the leaf to the dining room table because guests were coming over, and we were making room for additional guests. These items were stored in a special area, not to be confused, or used with day-to-day utensils. The other utensils were functional, and to be honest, the forks that we used during the week worked the same way. What made the Thanksgiving table setting different was it was set apart; we ascribed a difference to it. We made them special, we treated them differently, and we secured their value in velvet-lined drawers and a china curio. My parents also had dishes from older family members and thus the value of these items was priceless to us. We cared for these items because they were only used on special occasions.

Hence it is with sanctification. It is the setting apart and He is ascribing value to us for His use. But in a secular society only what I want is of importance. In this context, your importance is only as long as your lifespan. However, God's importance is for an eternity, and it can be passed down like fine flatware or china to another generation because the item has been kept and has been preserved and not overused. I would propose that the more we blend and become homogeneous and abandon our rituals of old, we will lose our significance. Without sanctification there is no legacy, it becomes the party of me, myself, and I, and that's not growth. I believe that secularism ends and begins with you, your wants and needs and that is a narrow view because those needs are always changing. But when you contrast sanctification, God is always adding new pieces to His china curio because He is preparing to serve many people. He's constantly adding pieces and buffing off those imperfections in our lives to make us better. Sanctification is the process of setting something apart so it can be used for a specific purpose that will have an impact beyond common use. Its design is special, distinctive and uncommon! It it meant to be noticed, observed, and respected. By sheer implication it is different from anything else.

God is jealous for us because He doesn't want the world and its contamination spoiling His prized possessions. He sets us apart, hides us in Him, and removes those items that are not pleasing. So, when we are placed on display the guests see the care and the difference between us and the everyday used items. However, the rejection of this precious attribute makes us brute, common, dull, and without a defined purpose. I believe that is why we keep changing our descriptive name tags because we are trying to define ourselves by ourselves which is impossible. We no longer have purpose, so we resort to labels and tags. Someone greater has to define us. But we rather self-identify, so sadly we re-name ourselves with each passing century settling for this rather than a divine mandate.

God's plan has always been secure from the beginning of time without alteration. He knows those who are His and He always knows what is best for us. We are not a party of one but of the family of God.

WHAT A JOY TO BE LOVED

August 30, 2021 entry: ... "and God said, because I told you so."

There are very few things in life that can press harder than when God is trying to tell you something to do. I was cooking one day, and God told me to call someone. Now I hadn't spoken to this person in quite a while, so I was going to prepare to settle in to make the call. It was a gentle thought that turned into an urging. So, I had planned to make the call during the course of the day. I went grocery shopping, tidied up the house, and did a few other things but I kept saying that I was going to make the call. I prepared dinner and the once gentle nudge was now a throbbing push. I kept saying, "I am going to." I ate dinner and then I made the call. In these situations, I am thinking, "is something about to happen?" "Is there a crisis and do I need to intervene?" All of these questions are running through my head, and I'm poised to react. I made the call, and well, it was, how can I say- uneventful. There were no fireworks, no crisis, no impending danger, no prayer request, no need, just a simple casual conversation for an hour and that was all.

After the phone call, I began to talk to God and ask Him the reason behind the urging for the call. I was befuddled by the urging and more questioning due to the outcome because it seemed like there was no reason behind the urgency. So, then I changed my posture, and said, "are you about to bless me for doing that?" Then God checked me in my spirit and said, "do I have to bless you for this, is this a tit-for-tat relationship? That behavior is what servants do they look for a return after each request." I then said, "No Lord that's not who we are, you don't have to pay me after each request that's not our relationship. I just wanted to understand what tonight was about…was it for me or was it for them?" God so took my breath away and left me in a pool of tears. He gently told me these simple words, "because I told you so." This simple statement changed the polarity of my thinking and put me seeing a God who knows and sees all yet seeks a relationship with us.

The request had really nothing to do with the phone conversation, rather it had to do with my response to His voice and His prompting. My prayer further unfolded that God's interaction with us as His children often requires us to do things just because He says so. There is no deep revelation, no mysteries to uncover, no realms to search. It's just a heavenly Father's interaction with His child and a child obeying His voice. This seems simple and without depth, yet how many parents struggle with compliance from their children?

In addition, what parent wants to pay their child every time they complete a task? These types of interactions are exchanges based on a monetary system, not a relationship based on love. His love for me is what compels me to act and obey.

After I reveled in the weight of this reality and understood the gravity of simple obedience; and before I could muster enough strength to get off my knees, I heard Him whisper this: "Be grateful that you hear my voice, there are so many people who don't." Wow! Oh, to be loved by God! God can invade our senses and push past all other distractions to make His voice distinct. Oh, to be able to hear and respond to the voice of the one who stills waters and makes mountains into prairies. His voice calms fear and establishes His promises to His children. His voice is without comparison and not being able to hear Him is my worst nightmare!

The love of any child is to hear their parent's voice and to respond to them, to engage and converse, and to have a relationship. That's how a bond is formed through talking which leads to knowing. I desire a deeper closer relationship, overall I just want Him to keep talking to me.

CAN I HELP YOU?

October 12, 2020 entry: "...the audacity not of power- but of help."

"Since you get more joy out of giving joy to others, you should put a good deal of thought into the happiness that you are able to give." Eleanor Roosevelt.

Eleanor Roosevelt was the wife of the 26th President, Franklin Roosevelt, and the longest-serving 1st lady of the United States serving for 3 terms or 12 years. Her tenure exposed her to wars, plight, depression, and uncertainty, yet she persevered even during personal struggles. Remarkably, access to power can produce two distinct responses: either self-indulgence or the need to help. Mrs. Roosevelt's life was centered on finding productive and lasting ways of using her influence and power to bring change to the poor, women, and youth, racial justice, and the fight for human rights. She used her office to press deep within the conscience of America and her allies to lift others from despair and to level set the arm of justice in varying arenas.

The act of being audacious requires boldness, tenacity, and reckless bravery toward a goal or a self-inspired ambition. But how many people have the audacity to help? Who has the drive every morning to help, inspire, and be bold and recklessly brave in our pursuit of this goal? Who has the targeted mindset to seek out a person(s) without regard for the general public or forgo personal desires to solve the problems of another? It's audacious in this season of personal fulfillment in every sphere of our lives to regard another with such passion; especially when we have to live our best lives ever. My grandmother who lived to be 103 years old would tell me that she wasn't satisfied until she did her "good deed" for the day. Being raised in a Missionary Baptist church she felt a Christian's responsibility was to relieve some measure of hurt or need from a person's life. So daily she would either visit/call a sick person; give financially to a cause; speak a word of encouragement; share her faith; help the helpless; or send a thoughtful card. But these things were her daily routine, and she wouldn't rest until she was certain that she helped someone that day.

I firmly believe that people are motivated by two things: money or vision. Yet even the wealthiest person has an urge to shed his/her wealth and give it to someone less fortunate. They realize that money doesn't produce the same stimulus that helping someone else does. The wealth of one doesn't have the same impact as helping hundreds or even thousands.

I believe it alludes to the need to be audacious to help! This time of uncertainty still resembles that of the 1930s when despair and the unknown hovered like black clouds, nevertheless, the opportunity to help was the light in a dark place. So, let's practice doing good! We cannot advert trouble or unpredictable tragedy, but we can produce avenues to relieve the hurt that trouble will produce. This is already in our imagination and our memory banks; we merely have to do it. So, let's be audacious.

WHO'S AFRAID OF THE BIG BAD WOLF?

February 16, 2021 entry: "You have to stand against the spirit of intimidation-whether loud or silent"

The story of the big bad wolf in nursery rhymes places the reader, which in most cases are children from ages 4-6 in a setting where the old hungry wolf is lurching to eat three pigs. Now based on which version you read; the three pigs end up in the home of the one smart pig who knew that the only safety from danger was in a home that was made with bricks. Yet, before we get to the part of the story about being safe from the wolf, the story immediately gives the reader the understanding that an enemy exists. The story would not be of any significance without the understanding that from the onset that there was opposition to the pigs' existence. It was the awareness that prompted the one pig to build and secure his safety. This is amazing how this fable is introduced to children at a young age unbeknownst to us. The context in our life experience is to be aware of the big bad wolf. Uniquely, the phraseology of the song, is rhetorical, "who is afraid", as if you should not be afraid.

Awareness of any impending danger actually lessens the impact of its damage. Because awareness is supposed to cause one to prepare against or defend oneself from the onslaught that the danger would bring. Throughout nature, we see animals that have self-defense mechanisms for their protection. They live with a heightened consciousness of possible predators, and this causes them to constantly be prepared for an attack. I would contend that intimidation is a signal for humans that danger or distress is nearby. Psychologists describe intimidation as, "the act of making others do what one wants through fear. Intimidation is a maladaptive outgrowth of normal competitive urge for interrelation dominance generally seen in animals, but which is more completely modulated by social forces in humans." I believe that the danger of intimidation lies in the fact that fear is doubled. Fear of intimidation and fear of what intimidation will bring. In most cases, the intimidator wins whether they intimidate quietly or loudly when a person succumbs to a perceived threat. Hence, causing the victim to surrender without defense or an action plan. This act rendered the answer to the question: "who is afraid? I am afraid." So, without engaging in any strategy we will allow our fear to make us fearful, and our fearfulness will cause anxiety and polarization, and polarization makes us an easy target.

However, history has proven time and time again that a good offense is a good defense. Intimidation is the signal to build the masonry wall around the items to be protected. To acknowledge the danger but appreciate the ingenuity that time and planning will provide for greater defense. Time to understand that a predator may only see from one direction- so pivot. Time to bring others to help fortify and support. Lastly, being aware the intimidator can also be defeated by a secure and well-crafted fortress. Remember, the wolf blew on a brick wall, and his breath had no power against it, and he left.

Intimidation is an indicator that you're valuable; so, don't run…build!

Leader's Self-Reflection

Identifying Your Current Mindset: Strategic Planning

Reflection is the first step in understanding where you currently stand. Here are a series of questions aimed at helping you identify your mindset:

1. Based on the prior entry, who is a person(s) that you can identify that you can go to in times of uncertainty?

2. In your industry, what is a danger that can compromise your organization, family, business? How are building a defense based on this awareness?

3. Share your strategy with your inner circle.

God Will Take Care of You

Be not dismayed whate'er betide,
God will take care of you;
beneath his wings of love abide,
God will take care of you.

God will take care of you,
through every day, o'er all the way;
he will take care of you,
God will take care of you.

Through days of toil when heart doth fail,
God will take care of you;
when dangers fierce your path assail,
God will take care of you.

All you may need he will provide,
God will take care of you;
nothing you ask will be denied,
God will take care of you.

No matter what may be the test,
God will take care of you;
lean, weary one, upon his breast,
God will take care of you.

© 1905 Martin' Walter Stillman Martin

DID I HEAR YOU CORRECTLY?

September 14, 2020 entry: "let us be keen to hear, not so much write or speak"

Growing up in a home where my father was an entrepreneur and pastor, and my mom was an English teacher, well let's say there was a lot of structure, rules, and social norms to be observed. My father served in the U.S. Navy, so we were instructed early on to respect our elders, only speak when spoken to, respect another person's property, keep our voice at a moderate level, not speak out of turn, and be wise once we spoke. These along with other traditional values were the measuring rod to determine if you were an honorable child.

Conversely, my mom was an honor English teacher who made sure that we conjugated every verb and noun. My siblings knew we had to have noun and verb agreement, or Mom was going to correct us immediately. We couldn't say, "I is going to the store," without Mom screaming, "I is?! We would quickly say, "I am going to the store." Geez. However, her love for proper English also gave way to additional grammar skills which was the art of context clues. Context clues are hints found in a statement or a paragraph that will give the reader insight into new words or meanings that they would not have originally known. She would constantly tell us to use our context clues when trying to solve an answer to things that were unknown in a situation or something we read. Now let me be clear because we were instructed not to speak as children doesn't mean that we weren't listening. My siblings and I ear hustled our way through our teenage years, then over time we were able to draw better conclusions from what we heard and observed. We began to piece things together a bit over time the more information we gathered. Sometimes our conclusions were correct, and sometimes they were dead wrong. Yet our mother didn't always give us the answer she would often refer back to, "use your context clues."

In times of crisis and uncertainty, we can quickly draw conclusions, assess recklessly, cast doubt, defame, and make rash decisions. Versus using context clues and listening in for what we don't know and information that we are unfamiliar with. One must first admit in any new situation that there are 3 striking components: a) I haven't been here before; b) I don't know what I don't know; c) Am I ready for more information than I currently have? Context clues require us to listen from a space of the unknown, so talking and writing have to be eliminated, and listening has to be at the forefront of the conversation. Then we can listen for gems and keys that will unlock the unknown. Too often in our current society, people are making judgment calls without the discipline of listening and waiting. It's a difficult pill in this current generation that the answer is not a search engine away. The art of context clues is not to redraw conclusions, but to wait for the next clue.

Just wait for it, the answer lies in the next conversation.

JUST STOP IT

June 30, 2021 entry: "We don't have to make any assumption about God...He is good!"

My grandmother was the daughter of a sharecropper, so I am literally 4 generations from slavery. This is an unbelievable reality while living in the 21st century. My great-grandfather's story is so compelling that there is not enough space in this entry to do it justice but let me conclude by saying that anyone could see the provision of God in his life. Now, this is difficult to imagine since at one point in his life he was a slave. Yet, his story did not encapsulate his time as a slave. His life was one of family, business, purpose, and perseverance. To be clear, I will not minimize the atrocities of slavery, the South, and the government that allowed it to exist. Yet, the highlight of his life was that "God is good." Surprisingly, the land that was left to him has been donated to build a church where slaves once worked.

Often when there is not a clear path or an immediate solution, the circumstance will take center stage and our visage reflects our emotions. Then our appearance will reflect in our decisions, and our decisions can alter our future. This is where we make judgment calls concerning everything around us and who is with us. This sense of being short-sighted is where many of us make mistakes. Trust me, I have been spiraled by life and have made rash decisions, even those I knew at the moment were bad. This is because we feel that doing something is more productive than doing nothing, even if something may render dire results. This is the insidiousness of the human condition. In our minds, something is better than nothing.

Yet, after living for a few years, I have discovered that this simple phase when declared with a pure heart, no pretension, or false platitudes centers and calms me. Simply, God is good. God's innate nature is good and not evil. His ability to be loving, kind, and most of all a good listener creates peace in dark hours. Imagine how many conversations He endures without complaint daily. Yet, He is open for another round of complaints day after day. But when we consciously consider that there is someone who may have a worse condition than we do, yet God patiently hears us, we can knowingly say that God is good. Surely, He could say, "Just stop it." But He doesn't. In fact, it is written in Holy Scriptures that, "He never slumbers or sleeps." Trust me I know when we hear complaints day after day, we want to scream, "Stop it," but we don't have the love and concern for mankind like God does, and that is one of the attributes that makes Him good.

Assumptions are never the platform that can couch any substantiated argument. This is because assumptions are based on unproven, weak, and questionable facts. But we don't have to assume about God, He does some of His best work in a crisis. Not that He caused the crisis. Rather, He is called upon during a crisis as if it were His fault; and He shoulders the problem as if it were His own. This fact alone proves His goodness. Never make assumptions about Him but acknowledge His goodness.

When I think of my great-grandfather, his life pales in comparison to mine in terms of my freedoms, luxuries, amenities, and comforts. He didn't live long enough to see his descendant's graduate college, racial integration, fair housing, the internet, or automation. Rather, his life was filled with manual labor, unfair treatment, misunderstanding, and grief. Yet, he had family, laughs, and a strong work ethic. Nevertheless, we agree on something that has lasted in my family longer than modern advancements. For centuries we declare that God is good!

DO YOU HAVE A BAND-AID?

June 18, 2021 entry: "God covers a situation, versus the devil who will leave an exposed open wound. God puts in the healing ointment, compress, and bandage. However, the devil will allow your injury to be exposed."

When I was growing up, I was a tad clumsy. Yes, they said I was accident-prone. There wasn't a step that I wouldn't trip over, a plate that I wouldn't break, or a bike that I wouldn't fall off of. It was sheer madness that anything that could be broken or tripped over was in my immediate path with my name on it. I thought for a time that I would be bound to eat off plastic plates for the balance of my life. I just didn't understand why my feet and hands were moving 20 seconds faster than my brain. Thankfully everything is in sync now.

When I was about 15 years old and my father who kept a pristine lawn was watering the grass on a summer day. We didn't have an automatic irrigation system, rather we had the old-fashioned green water hose. My dad would drape the hose over our chain-linked fence to make sure the front lawn was properly saturated. One summer day unbeknownst to both he and me, he pulled the water hose as I was jumping over it at the same time. I tripped and fell forward straight into our glass entry door; I tried to brace my fall with my right hand, but my hand went through the glass door shattering the glass and leaving glass in my hand and arm. When my father heard the crash, he came running around to the door as I was standing there in utter shock with blood running down my arm. The first thing he did was grab a towel and cover my arm and apply pressure to it; then he rushed me to the hospital where I had to get 12 stitches on the front of my arm and 6 on the inner part of my arm. Uniquely, he didn't make the door his priority, his first call to action was to cover the wound. Even at this moment, it is a faint memory of how the door got repaired.

I hope it's obvious the way that I am weaving the point of this writing with the life example above. In times of hurt and pain, God covers us first. Now, this doesn't mean that the wound is healed, at the moment the urgency is to cover it. The covering and applying pressure with compression allows the blood flow to stop and healing to begin. The function of the body is to stop excessive bleeding so a clot can begin to heal, and this is done by applying pressure. The pressures of life can start the process of healing to a cut or infected area that we have experienced. But God does this while we are covered, the pressure applied stops the blood flow, and then He can start mending that area. It's difficult to see at the moment how pressure brings healing, but without the pressure, we would bleed out and die. It is in the pressure of life with God covering us that we become stronger, the injured area is apparent, and God can start the healing.

What's always constant in our journey of life is there will be times that we trip and fall and have injuries. But be careful who is laughing when you fall. The devil always seeks to expose us at our weakest and most vulnerable moments. Without fail, he likes to sell tickets and have an audience at our demise and a laugh at our expense. Yet, our Heavenly Father picks us up, covers us up, applies ointment, and applies gentle pressure to transition us to healing. It is this attention to detail that saves our lives, establishes our next step, and gives us hope to go further.

WHAT TIME ARE YOU GETTING UP?

December 20, 2020 entry: "Some things look good not because they are good, but because they are platformed on a good foundation. It is not so much the work, as it is the prep work"

I have shared a few antidotes of my early childhood, and even though I didn't appreciate the rigor or discipline then, I see a major payoff as I have gotten older. Part of our family tradition growing up was to host large holiday parties with family and friends. We knew that on July 4th and Thanksgiving, we were sure to have at least 30 people over for dinner. My father was a superb cook, and he was known for his ribs, turkeys, desserts, and the fixings in between. He made our guests feel welcomed and everyone left with full bellies, good laughs, and a sense of true friendship. As children, we loved the have our friends over and with each "ding dong" of the doorbell we were so excited to see who was coming in next. Days before the holiday we would call our friends and talk about what we were going to play, eat, and talk about on that day. However, no one was coming over until my Mom made sure that the house was spotless before our guests came over.

The process of cleaning was intense. It was weeks in advance, we got up early in the morning, and there was attention to every little detail. My siblings and I cleaned the baseboard, polished the fine silver, cleaned the walls and wallpaper, re-lined the cabinet shelves, waxed the basement floor, and washed windows. I think you get the point! I would often think and sometimes say, "Momma no one is going to look in there." But she was not moved by our frustration, and she would say, "You never know what may happen." She knew two things: wandering eyes do look and never skimp on the necessary details. So, for us to host we had to do the prep work in advance, so when our guests arrived the food presentation was presented in a home prepared to receive them. How many of us have been turned off at a restaurant not because of the food but because the presentation was so disgusting that we left the establishment or never frequented it again?

Life can be filled with two types of people. People who have been prepped by a prior generation and those who have not. Now I am not talking about military discipline, I am referring to a generation who clearly understood that one day your child may be hosting. That hosting may range from dating to employment, from social interactions to social responsibilities. At some point inextricably there will be a fleeting moment when a person will tie your behavior to your childhood and how you were raised. Please note that

I know that this statement is not absolute: good parents can have wayward children, and those who lack parenting skills can have overachieving children. Yet, at some point, somebody somewhere was doing a little prep work in the life of a child. It is this work that is the foundation for what happens next. We can never assume that we become anything solely by our own doing and our own ingenuity. Rather what's being displayed in our lives is the foundation that we were built on. However talented, gifted, exceptional, or motivated there was someone behind the scenes who applied prep work to the talent.

This prep work is done early and with purpose. Fishermen bait fish early, construction workers start before the heat of the day, and farmers till the ground and feed the herd early, the point is that whatever we do for sustainability must be done early. This process gives the processor time to see and correct the error, reset the mold, and set the foundation properly. My mother started the process of cleaning weeks before the event, and if we are to yield productive citizens we must begin early before the mold hardens and the imperfect shape takes place. I dare not imply that this is a silver bullet, but I will contend that when I see giftings and talent, I don't look at the person as much as the foundation that they are standing on. When I look at any successes in my life, I cannot solely attribute them to my hard work or tenacity. No, I thank God for parents who had the foresight and got up early to do prep work.

I AM GOING WHERE YOU'RE GOING

November 24, 2020 entry: "If you are a teacher, students do what you say, but if you are a leader people do what you want; there is a collective buy-in.

There are many teachers that I have contact or professional interactions with. This profession is so vital to the human and national experience. These gifted individuals are undervalued and underpaid because what is the true value of having the ability to convey knowledge and principles to a person? As a daughter of a schoolteacher, I saw the rigor that goes into trying to make a subject matter achievable for all of your students. When did we start believing that every student learns at the same pace and style? When did we formalize our thinking to believe that creativity must be substituted for technology? These constant adaptations require teachers to be almost a chameleon by changing with each administrative shift. Yet, these noble individuals make the changes, adapt to new policies, and bring new systems to the classroom and the child is none the wiser about the stressors of the profession.

The true art of teaching is getting the student to do what you say and do it the way it was instructed. It is fascinating that one of the mystical things of education is that we put a child in front of a total stranger and by the sheer strength of their profession a child is to totally acquiesce to what they say and instruct. Think about it: there are no family ties, prior introduction, tea dates, family dinners, etc. No, it's merely, "this is Mrs. Jones, and do what she tells you to do." The art of getting a child to comply and believe in what is being taught is an ancient gift reserved for those who dare enter the hallowed halls of education. Teachers have the responsibility and privilege of shaping, molding, and preparing a child to be a productive citizen. With this distinct superpower, students submit like Superman to kryptonite, by just following the instructions and tasks given. This exchange between student and teacher often produces statements later on in life that, "Mrs. Jones was my favorite teacher."

Though it is honorable and expected to follow instructions, could the next step be for the student is to become more introspective and buy into the reasoning as to why the instructions were given? Could there be an evolution from instruction to intuitiveness? I think this is where teaching ends and leading begins. Being a leader is not merely giving instructions but the grace that others will buy into your vision and work alongside you to accomplish a task. This is where I believe it becomes a collective boat rowing and we're going in the same direction, rowing at the same pace without additional instruction, pushing against the same waves, and arriving at the same place at the same time. So, when does this process occur? I believe it begins when the leader makes the vision or the task so enticing and palatable that not being a part of it would be criminal. I believe that a leader can draw a description and paint a picture that is so clear that the student sees themselves as a part of the canvass. Sometimes a student cannot see themselves in the curriculum, so they fail the subject. But when a student sees themselves as a part of it, then this evolves into leadership, because leading has reproductive qualities. Leaders reproduce and multiply so that those who are led bring others with them and they see themselves as part of the canvass as well. This is when you see people following others, not because of a groupie session, but because they can see themselves in the project and being successful in it. It moves from yours to ours. This movement creates word connections like a team, we, family, unit, core, and fellowship. There is an abandonment of the singular and emphasis is on the plural. Leaders create opportunities for expansion, growth, stability, and individual creativity; and those who are a part see themselves as part of the whole.

Leaders create opportunities for a collective buy-in, not just instructions. They project ideas and adventures beyond our current comprehension and without detailed bullets, individuals find solutions to problems and pathways to success. So, the next time you hear someone say, "I am going where you are going" consider whether you have just entered the role of a leader.

Leader's Self-Reflection

Identifying Your Current Mindset: Who's Following you?

Reflection is the first step in understanding where you currently stand. Here are a series of questions aimed at helping you identify your mindset:

1. Looking back at your life, what type of people do you naturally attract? Do you know why this is?

2. What is your inspiration and is this transferable to others?

3. How much time do you spend with those individuals who are inspired by you? What do you do consistently to cultivate them?

I WANT TO BE WHERE YOU ARE

December 2, 2020 entry: "We can walk in the presence of God, and it will be all over us- His glory will be on us. We can't see it, but people can."

There is something glorious about morning dew. I love to get up in the morning and walk in the grass to begin an early morning grass watering. It makes the grass greener and lusher, and the birds come to feed early before the heat of the day to feed on seeds and worms. As I walk through the grass the cool wet feeling across my toes and ankles has a refreshing and cooling feeling. However, the most remarkable thing is to see how much dew and moisture attaches to you without you even noticing. Astonishingly, you may not see the dew, but the dew remarkably attaches itself, and it's evident that it is there. Whether it's on a leaf, a blade of grass, your hair, or your vehicle, dew has an attachment quality that all can see. But there is another quality of dew, which is its ability to change from one composition to another. Water can change from vapor to liquid which allows plants to cool down on a hot day, it is the same way that sweat cools down the human body.

Such is when we walk in the presence of God. Dew is akin to God's presence He is radiant, potent, and has a magnetic ability. When we enter into the presence of God, His glory or anointing is attached to us. You cannot walk into His presence and not be affected or changed. Conversely the same applies when negativity, doubt, anger, and bitterness are connected to us. Instead of radiating we repel; versus compelling, we confuse. Because anything that has magnetic abilities attracts elements that are magnetized by it. We must be aware and conscious not to allow our day, emotions, and behavior to be magnetized by pulling someone else into a negative space.

As leaders we have the awesome ability to change lives, organizations, and communities. Yet this ability must be tempered by the knowledge that like dew people are attached to us. Often their hopes, dreams, career objectives, and personal callings are connected to our ability to be a resource to them. It is with this understanding that we exchange with them and often we can change our composition like dew to meet their needs. We can be like a vapor hovering over them as a guide and a presence. Or we may need to be liquid that can either wash, refresh, or water seeds that have been planted in their lives. We must never discount our responsibility or this privilege. In the same way that the presence of God is on our lives we in turn must transfer and have thumbprints on another person's life.

It is not enough for them to advance our goals, if we in turn do not understand that our responsibility is to push every person assigned to, magnetized by, or lead by us further along than when we met them. It is this magical aspect of direct contact with dew that we must grasp as leaders. Please note that dew is in essence hydration. This is what the essence of a leader is. We must be hydration in the lives of those we lead, our communities that we serve, and a conduit for generations to come. Do not lead if you cannot water dry places in people, communities, or organizations. Our charge is to be change agents, and like dew we should impact every surface that we come in contact with.

WISDOM QUOTES

"Be the change you wish to see in the world." — Mahatma Gandhi

"The only true wisdom is in knowing you know nothing." — Socrates

The journey of a thousand miles begins with one step." — Lao Tzu

"If you don't stand for something, you will fall for anything." — Malcolm X

"In three words I can sum up everything I've learned about life: it goes on." — Robert Frost

"Happiness is not something ready-made. It comes from your own actions." — Dalai Lama

"Education is the most powerful weapon which you can use to change the world." — Nelson Mandela

"Don't go where the path may lead, go instead where there is no path and leave a trail." — Ralph Waldo Emerson

Milton Keynes UK
Ingram Content Group UK Ltd.
UKHW030738071024
449371UK00005B/362